Strategies for cash building

HOW TO MAKE A GOOD LIVING ONLINE

Copyright © Peter Kalmer, 2023

Table of Contents

STRATEGIES FOR CASH BUILDING
HOW TO MAKE A GOOD LIVING ONLINE

Introduction

5

Even if we live in a world full of unpredictability, there is one thing that we can say with absolute certainty: that the going is rough right now. On pretty much every front, inflation is picking up steam. You're working your tail off to make ends meet, but just when you think you're making some headway, life tosses a curve ball at you that strikes you out at home plate.

The accumulation of bills, the ongoing increase in the cost of essentials, and the ongoing fluctuation in the price of gasoline all contribute to a worsening financial situation. You have reached a point in your life where the job you do for a living feels like it is digging you deeper into a pit from which you cannot escape.

Please, Draw Some Air Into Your System... Calm down... and read the report that is going to be provided for you as this will help you understand that there is a solution to this exasperating circumstance that you have found yourself in. It is possible to make a living doing something that will not bury you like an avalanche. You have the ability to lift yourself up and look out at the same heartening sunshine that others have witnessed.

You can take solace in the fact that quieting your mind is within your reach, and we'll demonstrate how to do so by guiding you to internet sources of revenue.

Taking Down Myths

Given that we are discussing the possibility of making a living online, it is critical that concerns around internet fraud be addressed. When determining the course of action for your internet business, while it is important to be knowledgeable, there is no reason to let uncertainty stand in your way.

In today's day and age, the term internet is practically synonymous with cons, spam, and fraud. Simply due to the fact that it involves using the internet, most cynics look down on this method of earning a living. When they hear about any form of possibility to make money online, they will immediately cry "scam" or "fraud" from the rooftops.

In spite of the fact that there are con artists operating in the online business arena, there are a great many genuine chances waiting to be discovered. If you do some research, you will find a lot of information and recommendations that will help you recognize these cons, which will allow you to take the next step toward making a living from the convenience of your own home.

People are understandably leery of participating in any activity that takes place online due to the proliferation of con jobs and fraudulent activity over the entirety of the internet over the past several years. There are genuine ways to generate money online, and a lot of individuals have already done so effectively and continue to do so even today. You can be one of them! Therefore, you shouldn't let any lingering uncertainties cause you to miss out on this opportunity.

This study will show you how to make money in a lawful manner and how to avoid falling victim to dishonest schemes that could take advantage of you. When looking for an online business, your level of confidence will increase according to the amount of knowledge you have on cons that can be found on the internet. Gain the upper hand and take charge of the direction your company is heading in before someone tries to take advantage of you in business. Let's debunk some of those urban legends about cons!

The following are some of the most common statements made by most fraudulent websites, along with the truths that lie behind them:

It's a Myth That You Can Make Money Overnight – These cons will convince you that you can earn money even while you are resting. They make it seem as though attaining something requires very little effort on the recipient's part.

Truth: Although accomplishing this goal is not impossible, doing so will need a lot of toil and commitment on your part before you can lay claim to this accomplishment. The vast majority of online businesses require an initial investment of time before they can be considered profitable, but this investment will ultimately be worthwhile.

The expression "Turn your Computer into a Money Making Cash Machine!" is a Myth.

In point of fact, there are a lot of comments that begin with some sort of sales pitch like this one.Be wary of a pitch for a product or service that begins with such a remark, even if the statement itself is accurate. The majority of online business opportunities consist on selling the actual business. Con artists typically offer the benefit of making more money. In such a scenario, there is almost never any commercial value, at least not to you. Swindlers make money when people fall for their schemes and pay them for services or goods that they never intend to provide.

Myth: "Start your business for free! There is no money involved!" They promote the idea that you can get a business up and running with zero financial investment in the form of start-up fees.

Truth: Scams of this type will make a big deal out of the fact that there is "no money involved," but then they will ask you to give them a set amount of money in exchange for knowledge on how to start a business for free. They seem to be in conflict with themselves, doesn't it? There will be expenses incurred in the first stages of a new venture, but those expenses almost never exceed the available capital.

Myth: "Start Earning a Living from Typing at Home" This statement is comparable to a number of others that are plastered over the internet saying that you can start a business from home using your typing skills, or in some cases, data entry skills. However, neither of these things is true.

The truth is that it is possible to earn money from home by performing tasks such as typing or data entry, but not with men. It is in your best interest to provide these services to clients on your own rather than paying the con artists for the information on how to carry them out. You can learn how to accomplish it by doing your own study, and doing so is completely free!

There are a great number of additional avenues for fraud, but they should provide you with some insight into how such cons operate and the types of people they target most frequently. Always be aware of the various possibilities available to you, and don't be hesitant to investigate any possibility that makes you feel uneasy.

Getting Started

People have a tendency to put off beginning their own businesses out of worry that they won't be able to successfully navigate the process of getting things off the ground. The majority of the time, these individuals' apprehension can be attributed to the simple fact that they are unsure of how to complete the task at hand or even where to get started. You may put your worries to rest and breeze through the stage of getting started with the assistance of this report, which will offer you assistance with this procedure.

Let's begin with some often asked questions that the vast majority of newcomers have when they are beginning the process of doing something for the first time.

"Do I have to have special skills or degrees to start my own business?"

You will need to have some understanding in the industry you are going to embark in, but it is not required to have any business or academic degrees to achieve beginning your own firm. Obviously, this will be determined by the kind of company that you are interested in beginning.

In the majority of instances, conducting some straightforward research into the industry that your prospective company will operate in will be sufficient to provide you with the information you require. If you wish to offer a service such as web design, etc., you should have some abilities in that field before attempting to establish your own firm.

In order to become an expert in a particular industry, college degrees and relevant work experience are always beneficial; but, in order to start your own online business, you typically do not need to have any degrees. Because knowledge is more powerful in the digital world, it is more necessary than ever to read anything you can get your hands on that is related to your industry.

"Will it Cost a lot of money?"

The initial financial investment required to launch a new online business is typically minimal. Most of the money you invest in it goes into purchasing a computer, setting up internet access, and designing a website. The kind of company that you intend to launch will determine the kinds of additional expenses that you have to pay.

Businesses in which you will sell products that you have made will require some money to fill the inventory items, but the internet is a terrific place to find amazing prices on items that can be used for this purpose. You will need to add software packages to the list of items that you need to purchase if you intend to offer a service such as website design for sale.

The majority of the time, you won't need to rush into your neighborhood bank and beg the teller to give you a loan. Find the best bargains on the things you need for the business you pick, and you won't have to worry about the interest rates that a loan would add to your budget. This is because you won't have to take out a loan.

"Will I still be able to start my own business online, even if I've never run my own business before?"

Absolutely. Without having any prior expertise in business, hundreds of Internet marketers have been successful in launching their own companies and making a name for themselves in their own industries. To reiterate, how much time and effort you invest in your research is the single most important factor in the outcome.

You may gain knowledge about every facet of the company that you want to launch by making use of the internet, which puts a wealth of relevant information right at your fingertips. Utilize this resource to your advantage in order to acquire the power that comes along with knowledge so that you may get what you want out of life. You can get advice, suggestions, and all kinds of information from individuals who have gone where you want to go and done what you want to do.

"How much money can I make from an online business?"

The answer to this question is going to depend on a great deal of different things. What kind of business you decide to launch, the amount of time and energy you put into it, and the rate of return on the products or services you provide are all factors that go into determining how much money you will ultimately bring in.

While some people who promote products or services on the internet make six figures a year, others make about the same amount as an employee at a fast food restaurant makes on average. You will always be in a better financial position than those people who have to drive a long distance to get to their work, regardless of how successful your firm is. The money that they spend on things like transportation, work attire, and meals, among other things, is money that ends up in your possession rather than the possession of another person.

"Do I really need a website?"

To run your business successfully, you will need to have a website. You are going to have to either sell your items or demonstrate to potential customers what services you can provide for them. You won't need to rent out pricey space in a physical building to use it for your internet business because it functions in the same way that an office or store would.

If you utilize one of the various website design software programs available or a website construction service, creating websites is not too difficult of a task. Don't let the fact that you don't know how to design websites stop you from starting a business because you can always hire a professional web designer to make a killer site for your company if you so want.

"Do I need special business licenses to run an online business?"

It is highly recommended that you get in touch with the relevant departments of your local government in order to find out what requirements are necessary in your region. Because the requirements for beginning a business in a given location may vary, it is important to do some preliminary research before getting started.

I'm nervous about taking money from customers. What if I mess up the payment processing system?"

If you are going to be selling products, you will need to use an online payment system such as PayPal or Clickbank. The entire payment procedure, including any necessary reimbursements, will be handled by these programs on your behalf. Take advantage of the possibility presented by the fact that shopping cart software typically comes packaged together with a web design application.

Different Types of Legal Online Businesses

When you first get started in the world of internet business, you have a few different options available to you to select from. Before moving on, it is strongly recommended that you investigate each available choice and determine which one best fulfills your requirements. The following is a list of some of the most common types of businesses that people start up on the internet, along with an explanation of what each one entails:

Service Based Businesses

When you run a company that provides customers with some kind of service, you have what's known as a "service-based business." Some examples of this are as follows:

- Writing

- Web Design

- Accounting/Bookkeeping

- Virtual Assistant

Other proprietors of small businesses find that they are unable to complete all of the necessary activities for their companies on their own, and as a result, they choose to contract out the work. They search for individuals who are capable of providing the services that they require to be carried out on their behalf.

If you have experience in any of these areas, you may start your own business selling yourself and give that experience as a service to others. For instance, if you have some experience writing and are able to write well, you may give your writing services to others who need writing done for their websites. This would be a good use of your writing skills.

What skills are needed?

You need to have a certain degree of expertise under your belt, and the quantity of skill you need depends on the type of service you want to deliver to potential customers. It is not necessary to have educational degrees in order to provide these services; nevertheless, clients do prefer to see that you have some kind of experience in order to do the duties that they require to be done.

Working online does not provide the opportunity for face-to-face interaction that is available to potential employees at traditional businesses. Because it is more difficult to establish trust online, employers want to ensure that the prospective employees have the necessary experience and education to accomplish the job.

Even while having more than ten years of experience in a particular field is not required to execute a job, the fact that you have done it in the past and have some testimonials to back up that claim helps a great deal.

What tools are needed?

The tools you need will depend on the type of services you plan to provide. The more common ones that most service based businesses should have are:

- Computer

- Reliable Internet access

- Phone

- E-mail program

- Website

Additionally, it is likely that some software applications will be available for purchase. Each service utilizes a variety of programs, some of which are unique to that service, but the majority of services require a word processing software, an excel application, and some services utilize a web design program.

You should give some thought to getting an Instant Messaging program for those customers who would prefer to be able to get in touch with you right away without having to use the phone to call you or wait for a response to an e-mail they sent you rather than having to do either of those things.

How do you get started?

Your first order of business should be to make a decision regarding the kind of service you intend to provide for your customers. Make a note of everything that comes to mind that demonstrates that you have some level of expertise or experience in the subject matter that is being discussed.

After that, you should get a website established for your business. Showcase your expertise or years of experience on your website, and make sure to include client testimonials from previous customers who have benefited from your services and been delighted with the outcomes. Include your pricing information here, as well as any other pertinent details regarding the operation of your company.

It is important to advertise your website in a variety of different online locations in order to raise awareness about your online business and make it easier for prospective customers to locate and investigate it. Reiterate to customers how the process will unfold whenever they contact you to employ you for a service, regardless of what it is they require. For instance, you should explain to them how they will be billed for the work that has been completed, as well as the amount that will be charged, etc.

You shouldn't expect to make a lot of money right away because it will take some time to develop a clientele of consistent customers; prepare yourself for this reality. Give it some time and maintain marketing your service-based business until you reach the point where you are almost having to turn away customers because you are too busy.

Those individuals who are currently providing the service at another employment may find that operating a business that is based on providing that service to others is an ideal career move for them. You have a better chance of making more money by providing such services online, rather than by working in a traditional storefront role.

Affiliate Marketing

It's an online business where you put your selling and marketing skills to use to get customers to purchase things manufactured by other people so that you may earn a commission off of the sale. You will typically receive a set amount of money based on the sales of those products that you make; however, in other instances, you may be able to earn money from the clicks from your site that drive the customers to the affiliate websites.

You might be able to make some money by encouraging people to join up for various products on the affiliate websites, such as newsletters and the like. When you sign up for an affiliate program, you should be sure to check out how their process works and each one will have its own unique way of explaining how it operates and what it entails. This will be monitored through the use of an affiliate link that will be provided to you so that you may place it on your website.

What skills are helpful?

To become an affiliate marketer, it is not necessary for you to have prior experience as a salesperson or in the marketing industry. However, having the knowledge necessary to carry out these activities is going to be very vital. Learn as much as you can about the inner workings of online marketing, as well as how to become a great affiliate marketer by listening to the experiences and advice of other successful marketers.

In order to make your business successful in the field of affiliate marketing, you will need to put in a lot of effort and a lot of dedication. Don't even think about making this your online business if you don't have the time or the gumption to put in the effort to make it successful.

What tools are needed?

The number of tools that will be required will be kept to a minimum. In addition to the standard necessities, such as a computer and dependable access to the internet, you will also need a website from which to sell the affiliate products. You won't have to purchase additional things simply so that you can sell them; you won't need to do that.

Your website is going to require new content on a consistent basis, so you should get ready to either write some of the articles on it yourself or hire someone else to do it for you. Having a blog that links to your website is another useful strategy for gaining favor with search engines and increasing your visibility online.

How do you get started?

For your website devoted to affiliate marketing, you will need to choose a specialized field, or niche. This helps you stand out from the crowd of other similar businesses. For instance, you could focus on nutrition as your particular area of expertise. After that, design a website that caters to the specific segment of the market that you decided to target with your company.

The next step is to locate things to sell as an affiliate that can be found on that site. Make sure that the products you choose to offer for your business are connected, even if only in some little manner, to the specific market segment that you have decided to target with your affiliate marketing endeavors.

If you have determined that the field of nutrition is where you want to focus your efforts, you should look for affiliate items that are connected to nutrition in some way. If you run a business and don't provide similar products, not only do you face the risk of giving the impression that you're not professional, but the search engines also won't be too happy with you.

There are a lot of people who are able to amass a respectable amount of wealth by operating this kind of company. It is essential to keep in mind that the bulk of your work in an enterprise of this nature will consist of marketing your website in an effort to attract customers. When they do find you, your website needs to be able to pique their interest in your products to the point that they will make a purchase utilizing the links you provide.

Selling on E-Bay

This is yet another common and successful online business that a great number of people commonly begin with. E-Bay is a well-known website that hosts online auctions, and millions of people use it on a daily basis to seek for things and make purchases as a result of finding good offers.

You can sell anything you have lying around your house in addition to selling things through a practice known as drop shipping. When you conduct a search on the website of eBay, you will see that users are selling a wide variety of goods and products. It's possible that they are used things or brand new items bought in bulk from wholesalers. In either case, individuals will be willing to pay a significant amount of money if you can provide them what they are looking for. Some people may go to great lengths, such as purchasing items from garage sales and flea markets, with the sole intention of making a profit by reselling them on eBay.

What skills are helpful?

To be successful in selling products on eBay, you don't need a whole lot of specialized knowledge or experience. The ability to successfully advertise your products is going to be the single most critical skill to possess. People will be able to locate the products you are selling by conducting a search on the website; however, if you want to make money in this kind of business, you will need to market those items in other places in order to get people to find them.

If you are selling stuff from your home, you should be able to snap a nice photo of the item so that others can see what shape the item is in.

What tools are needed?

To start a business of this nature, the one and only tool you should require is an account with eBay via which you can sell your wares. If you want to sell your products through a process known as drop shipping, you will need to find a wholesaler who will send the products to the end users on your behalf.

To accurately monitor your sales, you will need to have access to a computer that is connected to the internet via a dependable connection. In order to collect payments from your clients, you will require a web-based payment processor such as PayPal.

How do you get started?

Create an account with eBay that enables you to sell items on the platform, and then log in. Make it a point to shop on the site yourself in order to contribute to the growth of your user ratings and give potential customers a little more assurance when purchasing from you.

You should upload pictures of the things you are selling, if at all possible. Items with photos of the item tend to sell significantly more quickly than those without photos. People like to get a good look at what they're purchasing, so you should provide them the highest quality photo you can manage to post.
You may learn how to make more sales and how the process of selling on E-Bay works by reading all of the informational materials and rules that are available on the E-Bay website and reviewing them.

You can kickstart your very own internet business with great success by selling on eBay. You won't need a lot of expensive equipment to get started with this venture, so you can get your feet wet in the world of online business right away. In addition to this, you will be able to declutter your home by getting rid of stuff that are taking up unnecessary space while also making a little more money on the side.

Making money from Membership Sites

The sale of memberships to websites is a source of revenue for certain proprietors of internet businesses. People pay for memberships on websites so they may access exclusive content that is updated on a regular basis by the website's proprietor.

For online customers that are in need of content for their websites, for instance, you may sell memberships to your website. Depending on the length of time that your subscriptions are valid for, the memberships might need to be renewed every few months or so. When a member chooses to keep their subscription active, you are rewarded monetarily.

This is the kind of enterprise that has a decent chance of turning a profit. You won't spend a lot of money to provide your members with informational goods, but you could charge them a nice amount to access them, which would provide you a profit that would continue to accrue over time.

What skills are helpful?

Having experience in marketing will be of the utmost benefit. Bringing Internet users to your website where they can purchase memberships is the key to financial success on the Internet. For the sake of maintaining a positive user experience on your website, it would be beneficial to have some prior experience managing websites.

You should probably have some level of familiarity with the things that you are selling. For instance, if you provide your members with access to articles, you should be aware of the qualities that define a good article as well as the ways in which articles serve various functions.

What tools are needed?

To meet the requirements that running a membership site would place on your website, you will require one of excellent quality. There must to be good service in the event that something goes wrong with the site. There are a few applications for membership site management software that can assist you in getting one up and running for less than one hundred dollars.

Another item that you will require is content for the website. You have an obligation to offer fresh content that can be utilized on a regular basis to your paying members. Depending on what you intend to provide for your users, it can come in the form of written articles, computer applications, or even games played online.

How do you get started?

You will need to do some planning before you launch your membership website. What do you want to provide for the people who join your membership group? Are we talking about content, software, or something else entirely? As soon as you've settled on a decision, the next step is to think of a fresh and original perspective that you can offer your customers.

You may supply content in a specific field, such as nutrition, or you could provide a particular kind of written material; whatever it takes to give people who use the internet a new perspective, you could offer it as content. This helps you stand out from the sea of other businesses that are in the same industry as you.

Next, have a shopping cart function added to your membership website so that you can process payments for the various levels of membership. It is expected that the membership management software applications will come equipped with everything necessary for you to run your organization successfully. The only thing missing from your plan would be the actual material that you would distribute to your members.

The phase that is going to be the most crucial is going to be marketing your membership site in order to get people to find you. Later on in this study, we are going to talk about several marketing tactics.

You might be able to make an income that is similar to a passive one through the use of membership websites. People will have no trouble handing over their money to you to continue renewing their access to the content of your website if they are pleased with what you provide for them and the value they receive from it.

Making Money From Selling Products

It is possible to conduct business of this kind in a number of different ways. You could, for example, manufacture and market your own goods. This kind of business is frequently entered into by crafters in order to sell their own works to the general public on the internet. This is also the route that scrapbook creators choose to take for their businesses.

Using an online store that sells a variety of things is yet another method for marketing products. There would be no inventory of things for you to stock at your home, and there would also be no requirement for you to send anything directly from your own location. The products are ordered through the'store' that you have established, and the wholesaler that is delivering the products will ship the items directly to the clients on your behalf.

What skills are helpful?

The capacity to put in long hours and provide excellent service to customers are two of the qualities that you should possess. A significant portion of your time will be devoted to marketing your websites in the hope that they will be discovered by prospective clients. To supply the clients with all of the information they require while determining whether or not to purchase your products, it will be vital to have a website that has been put up well.

Because customers will ask questions about the products and can come to you with issues that need solving, having strong customer service skills will be essential to your success in this line of work. Getting to know your consumer well and developing a positive rapport with them will pave the way for them to return to your business and purchase additional items. You may assist yourself achieve that goal by giving them the highest-quality customer service possible.

What tools are needed?

If you want to sell products that you have created yourself, you will need to build up an inventory of the components that you will need to produce those products. If you want to save some money, it is in your best interest to do some shopping around and find some good discounts on things that can be bought in large quantities.

Your customers will need to be able to locate your products, understand what they are, and place orders for what you are selling, so obviously you will need a website to facilitate all of these things. Make sure the website you're using has a shopping cart option so that your company's purchasing procedure will be streamlined.

How do you get started?

The very first thing you are going to want to do is make a decision about what it is that you are going to offer for sale. Are you planning on selling your own things that you've created, or do you intend to sell other people's products by utilizing drop shippers?

If you want to sell things that you make yourself, then you will need to do some research on different suppliers to get the materials that you will need to create those products. Have some already made up so that when customers begin to place orders for your goods, you will be able to ship them out immediately rather than making them wait an additional day or two while you make them up.

After you have finished the planning stage, the next step is to construct a website where you may sell your products. Make sure the site can be navigated easily and isn't too distracting for the user, as this could result in them losing interest in your company very quickly.

Marketing your items is the final stage in getting started in this business, and that topic will be covered in more detail later on in this study. Do not skip this stage because it is the most critical one if you want your business to be successful and you should not be sloppy with it.

Selling your own wares on the internet is a great method to get some extra cash. There is no reason why, if you currently make things that you give away as presents to friends and family, you shouldn't take the product to the internet and start selling it there.

If you like the idea of selling products, but don't want to create one to make yourself or if you just don't feel like you are creative, then you can still achieve this kind of business by having someone else ship products for you. If you don't want to create one to make yourself or if you just don't feel like you are creative, then this is an option for you. You will have the freedom to spend the necessary time with your family if you get started in this manner online; nonetheless, you will still be able to earn a living.

Making money the PLR way

Paid Label Rights is what "PLR" stands for in this industry's lingo. It is written content that can be sold to other people so that those other people can use it for whatever purpose they see fit to use it for after purchasing it. Website proprietors look for these kinds of resources in order to acquire content for their websites at a price that is more affordable.

When stated in such a manner, it does not sound like a lucrative business prospect. The fact of the matter is that a single collection of written material can be repackaged and resold to a great number of different individuals. The process is explained in more detail below.

Take, as an illustration, the scenario in which you are selling a collection of ten articles, each of which is centered on a certain subject, such as the care of pets. These bundles are often offered for sale at a price of approximately one dollar per item. Someone who maintains a website concerning the care of pets will purchase a package from you in order to obtain content for inclusion on their website. You just made $10.

Now, that identical set of 10 different items can be sold repeatedly after being packaged together. You could make a grand total of $500 from the sale of that one bundle if you sold the same 10 articles 50 times, bringing the total amount of money you made from that package to $500. Your possibility for making a profit may significantly increase if you sold more than one package of PLR articles at the same time.

Everyone has its own unique pricing structure, and they each provide a varied variety of PLR content in addition to a selection of unique article subjects. Along with articles, you also have the option of selling material in the form of e-books and special reports. People are free to take these articles, adapt them to their own requirements, and use them however, whenever, and anywhere they like.

What skills are helpful?

Writing abilities are a pre-requisite for this position. Even if the people who buy your articles will probably change them anyway, you will still need to write articles of a high quality for them. You may hire a ghostwriter to write them for you, but keep in mind that you would have to pay them for their time. This is a fantastic alternative to consider if you don't mind giving up some of the profit in exchange for their services.

It is also vital to market the content you have available for PLR license. You will need to get people to find your content in order to make decent money in this business. Because of this, you should pull out all the stops when you first begin this business in order to maximize your chances of success.

What tools will I need?

If you plan on writing the content of the post yourself, you will want a computer that has word processing software already installed on it. You will also require a website in order to sell your PLR content online.

If you decide to pay someone person to write the content for you, you will need to search for a ghostwriter who is within your price range and produces high-quality work.

How do you get started?

Getting the articles written up will be the first step in getting this project started. You will want to make sure that the collection of articles that you are going to sell together all have some sort of connection to the subject that you have chosen to focus on as the overall theme. Gardening, taking care of pets, proper nutrition, physical activity, and other related topics could be discussed.

Make a decision regarding the price at which you will sell the articles, and then prepare a website from which you may conduct the sale. You can certainly use a website that offers the service of selling them for you, but it is recommended that you sell them from your own website and handle the marketing on your own.

If you decide to go into this kind of business, you may make a lot of money selling PLR because there are millions of websites on the internet that need material. You may easily provide a comfortable living for yourself and your family if you have a solid understanding of how to sell your products and services effectively.

Make Money From Selling Informational Type Products

When it comes to making money off of your expertise, the internet is an excellent venue. There are a great number of people who are willing to pay practically any price in order to obtain the knowledge that they have been searching for for so long. You have the potential to bring in a significant amount of money if you possess the expertise that they are searching for.

Informational products come in many forms. It could be one of the following:

- E-Books

- E-Courses

- Tutorials

- Guides

- Podcasts

These are well-known informational items that are in high demand all over the world among people who utilize the internet. If you feel that you have something important to say, then this may be the right line of work for you.

What skills are helpful?

You should be well-versed in the subject matter that you are going to discuss with your target audience. To be able to perform this, you won't need a PhD degree or any other type of advanced education, but it will help if you have a fair level of information about the subject area.

The capacity to promote your materials effectively will also be of great assistance. The more people you can reach with your products, the more people there are who could be interested in purchasing from you.

What Tools will be needed?

The equipment you need to bring will be determined by what it is that you intend to provide. E-books and Guides could be authored on word processing software and then converted to a PDF document, which is the most popular sort of document that consumers demand.

For the development of effective e-courses, the utilization of autoresponder software is essential. In order to produce podcasts, audio recording and editing software is required. There are a few distinct approaches that may be taken while constructing a tutorial. When presenting your material, you have the option of using either a PowerPoint presentation or software designed specifically for video tutorials. Video tutorials are an excellent method for walking customers through each step of utilizing a particular program, and they may be found online.

Websites and blogs will be essential to the promotion of your informational items from, respectively.

How to get started

Your product will require that you settle on a subject matter for it. Which of the following do you know the most about, and which of these subjects can you best serve the needs of your prospective customers? After you have determined the information that you wish to deliver, you should conduct research on the subject at hand to determine whether or not you are able to provide the information in a manner that is fresh and original.

You will need to come up with something fresh to offer your consumers as a free gift as there are already a great number of electronic books, courses, and other digital products available for purchase on the internet. If they don't think you have something new to offer them, they won't be as prepared to part with their money as they otherwise would be.

First jot down or record your informational product, and then revise both of them till they meet your standards. When you are certain that it is exactly how you want it, you can then begin marketing and selling it. You can sell it online by starting a website or a blog, and you should make sure the content of your

---

website's web copy attracts the attention of internet users so that they would buy what you are selling.

If you are able to do so, it would be in your best interest to have the promotional copy for such products written by a professional copywriter. They are able to write material in such a way that makes your product seem irresistible to potential customers and encourages them to buy it.

Making educational items won't set you back a lot of money, but selling them will bring you a healthy profit for your business. This is a wonderful method to generate revenue online while having a flexible schedule, which enables you to spend more time with your family and gives you more freedom.

Make Money Blogging

Blogging was originally conceived as a medium through which individuals may make connections with one another and exchange photographs, stories, and experiences. It was seen to be an excellent personal journal type tool that one could use in order to make their imprint on the internet through the many experiences that they had.

After that, blogs progressed to become both effective marketing tools and a channel through which users might generate revenue for themselves. Blogging may be a lucrative source of money in a number of different ways. Here are some of them:

If you have a website or blog, you may use the top search engines' Adsense program to earn a little additional money on the side. The concept is that you put these adverts on your website, and whenever a user clicks on one of those ads coming from your website, you are paid a certain amount of money. The more clicks you can generate from the people that visit your website, the more money you will make. Before you enroll in any of their programs, it is important to familiarize yourself with what behaviors are prohibited because there are some guidelines to follow if you decide to choose this path.

Product Reviews: There are some websites that allow you to sign up and become a member, and doing so can help you connect with other businesses that are looking for individuals to review their products and give them some publicity on your blogs. In most cases, the primary qualification for this is to have a blog that has been in existence for some time and receives a satisfactory number of readers. If you were to write a review of their product on your blog, each of those companies would pay you a certain amount.

Contextual Links - Some website or business owners may pay a blogger to include one of their links within the content of the blogger's blog entries. It's possible that the blog's owners are the ones reaching out to the author, but it might also be a corporation that's playing the role of an intermediary. These corporations will discover blogs that are pertinent to their company websites, and as a result, the links that are supplied on the blogs will be pleasant to search engines. This is an excellent strategy for bringing in additional visitors to a website.

Blogs provide yet another venue from which one may profitably market and sell their own wares. Blogs are used extensively by entrepreneurs who sell home décor items or food container items online to help sell their products and generate more revenue.

What skills would be helpful?

The ability to market your blog is the primary talent required for this kind of business, but there aren't many others. To ensure the success of your blog, you should do as much research on the topic as is humanly possible and familiarize yourself with various blogging best practices.

What Tools would be needed?

A blog, in addition to a computer equipped with an internet connection, would be your primary instrument for this endeavor. There is a wide variety of software for creating blogs available on the market today. While others demand a payment on a regular or yearly basis before you can begin using their services, some don't charge anything to get started with their platform.

Paid versions of blogging applications provide you access to additional features that might help you connect with other bloggers and improve the number of people who visit your blog. Because the free versions are so simple to set up and the most of them are so well-liked by bloggers, it shouldn't be too difficult to locate individuals with whom you may make connections.

How to get started

Sign up for a program that manages blogs and start contributing entries to the one you choose. Make it a point to post to your blog on a consistent basis, preferably twice a week at the very least. Blogs that aren't updated on a consistent basis have a greater likelihood of disappearing into the void of the internet.

You should try to get as many people to read your blog as feasible. To increase the amount of people who see your blog, you should get it listed in blog directories, join the blog rolls of other people's blogs, and leave comments on the posts that other people's blogs authors have written. The more people you are able to persuade to visit your website or blog, the better your chances will be of turning blogging into a profitable way to make money.

The majority of blogging systems will have a sign-up for AdSense advertisements already integrated in their setup feature, making it simple to get started with that feature. This will make it easier to monetize a blog. If you want to provide product reviews and contextual links on your blog, you will need to have been writing for some time and have a significant volume of visitors coming to your site.

Identify the firms that will help you connect with businesses that want to pay to have their products reviewed on your blog or have their links embedded with your blog post entries when your blog is ready. When your blog is ready, find the companies that will help you connect with these businesses. After you've completed those steps, you'll be able to utilize your blog to generate a supplementary income for yourself.

If you are willing to put in the effort to market your blog, you can generate some additional income with relative ease through blogging. Those that are successful at blogging for financial gain employ every strategy available to them in order to make their blog well recognized in the communities that exist on the internet. Those who do not have this ability typically earn no more than a few cents per week at most.

Make your blog more than just a leisure activity you engage in every once in a while; elevate it to the level of a profitable business venture. Become one of the most successful bloggers. It will be beneficial to both your wallet and your credit score.

Making Money Coaching Others

A coach is someone who shares their expertise in a particular craft with others who wish to achieve the same level of success that they have in that profession. It's possible to be an expert in anything, from writing to marketing to the business of coaching itself.

You may become a coach pretty easy and make money doing it if you already have a lot of expertise or knowledge in a particular field. There are many coaches who also aid others in the fields of web design and graphic design, as well as in the field of coaching itself.

A coach would guide newcomers in that field through the learning process by guiding them through various tips and strategies and answering queries.

What skills are helpful?

The capacity to be a good listener is the most vital quality you need have for this kind of business, so make sure you work on developing it. You should also possess a lot of patience when dealing with customers. Those who employ you as a coach want you to listen to their negative experiences and assist guide them out of the mud they find themselves in, regardless of how weird those experiences may sound to you.

If you want to build relationships with people and establish your reputation in this industry, you should have a solid understanding of your profession. Being a web designing tutor would not be a smart option if you have never developed a website in the past. Your lack of experience will be noticed right away, and people will lose trust in you as a result.

What Tools will be needed?

You should have the following in this kind of business:

- Computer

- E-Mail program

- Website

- Informative content for your site

- Shopping cart feature for your site to handle payments

- Telephone dedicated for business purposes

There is a good chance that the majority of your interactions with customers will take place through the use of your e-mail programs; however, there are some customers who may feel more at ease being able to have a conversation with you on a more one-on-one basis, which is why you should include a phone in your arsenal of tools.

How to get started

Prepare a strategy for your company. In what capacity will you be supplying a service in which you have expertise? To assist in establishing your company as an authority in its field and to develop credibility, have some articles and other forms of written material created for your website.

Describe the process your service follows and the fees that will be charged on your website. Show some testimonials from other people who have utilized your services in the past and have been satisfied with the outcomes. Make sure that your website is simple to navigate so that those who are looking for information about your coaching business won't get lost.

Your clients will come to you if you market your coaching business properly. Plan the objectives that the customer hopes to accomplish by working with you, and then have a conversation about how those objectives might be achieved. Pay attention to their concerns and inquiries, then provide enlightening responses and ongoing assistance so that they can continue making progress toward their objectives.

On the internet, those who have a lot of expertise or a lot of knowledge in a particular field are in high demand as coaches. Make use of what you know about a subject and offer a coaching service to others so that you can assist them in becoming an expert in the same field as you are.

Make Money in the Genealogy Business

Those individuals who have a passion for ancestry and enjoy researching our family history will find this to be an ideal prospect for a business venture. Genealogists make their profession by compiling family trees for clients who either lack the time or the persistence to undertake the work themselves.

The majority of people are curious in their family tree and the actions taken by their ancestors that may have had a lasting impression on the globe. By conducting the research for them and giving them with information about their family history, you may capitalize on their natural curiosity.

What skills would be helpful?

A strong emphasis will be placed on your ability to investigate topics thoroughly and organize information effectively. Genealogy is a discipline that emphasizes the development of these talents. You will need to be aware of where and how to conduct research on the ancestry of each family and be able to provide the results in a way that is simple enough for your consumers to comprehend.

What Tools would be needed?

You will want a dependable internet connection in addition to a PC. In order to get the most out of your research on ancestry, you should sign up for subscriptions to some of the most reputable genealogical websites. You should also consider purchasing any research books or enrolling in some workshops to pick up some pointers and techniques for investigating family trees.

To operate your business successfully, you will require a website. Both the manner in which you carry out your business and the fees you charge will need to be communicated to clients. If you can, provide clients with some samples to demonstrate the thoroughness of your job.

How to get started

Gather all of your materials, and look for websites that specialize in genealogy that you can subscribe to. Make a website where you can sell your service, and after that, begin marketing your company so that customers will find their way to your website.

In addition to using the resources offered by local libraries, courthouses, and historical organizations, you should utilize the internet for your research. You could have to talk to several people in order to get the information you need, in which case you might have to look into a phone to utilize.

You can use software packages that supply that information for you to create a family tree document that will hold all of the information about the family heritage, or you can create your own family tree document.

If you enjoy doing research and have an interest in historical materials, then you should think about starting a business in this field. You may satisfy the need that individuals have to learn about their family history while also making money doing something that you enjoy doing.

Make Money with Desktop Publishing

If you're a creative person who's also good with computers, you should think about starting an internet business that involves desktop publishing. You may produce things like adverts, calendars, flyers, and brochures here.

Because each of these kinds of papers may be generated using a program or two on your personal computer, it is not necessary to have high-priced hardware in order to generate them.

There are a lot of individuals looking for these creative pages to use for a variety of different purposes, but they don't know how to make one for themselves. If you have any expertise in this field, you might put it to use to gain money by giving them with the aforementioned creations.

What skills are helpful?

You should be able to navigate your way around a computer and be familiar with a variety of software packages. This is one of the abilities you should have. Because of the prevalence of the usage of computers, having artistic talent is not essential to succeeding in this field.

What Tools are needed?

Besides a computer, you should have the following equipment:

- Desktop publishing software

- Photo editing software

- Laser or Color Printer

- Scanner

- High Quality printer paper

Make sure you know how to use all the features of your equipment well so you can provide the best quality service for your clients.

How to get started

You need to make sure that your company has access to all of the appropriate machinery. First, you should choose a certain market segment to concentrate your marketing efforts on, and then you should design your website so that it caters to that segment. Your website should display examples of your previous work to demonstrate your level of experience in the relevant sector to potential customers.

You might also improve your knowledge of desktop publishing by reading any of the available tutorials or guides on the subject.

Desktop publishing is a business that may be quite lucrative for anyone who enjoys the process of making masterpieces that can make other people green with envy. If you are one of those people and you are looking for something that will provide flexibility, then this company is one that you should investigate more.

Creating a business from unusual ideas

Creating an online business via more traditional methods is something that we've gone over already. There are also some unorthodox means that need to be taken into consideration. When we talk about ideas that are unorthodox, we're referring to those that have been proposed by individuals but have been met with derision from others. The individuals in question then carried those concepts to the pinnacle of success and generated a significant amount of money off of them. The following is a list of some of those concepts that most people believed would never come to fruition:

One person found a way to make a good living by locating and selling obsolete seminars that had originally been offered for a price of several thousand dollars.

Domain names: Someone had the bright notion that they could make money by providing a service in which they came up with domain names for other people and then charged them for the privilege. Although it may sound absurd, the company began to thrive after they made the change. It turned out that a rather significant number of people required such service.

Someone who ended their engagement, got the ring back, and then discovered that they couldn't return it for its full value is rumored to have been the inspiration for the business model of selling used engagement jewelry. They created a website that allows individuals who are in the same predicament as them to sell their jewelry and get back the amount that they initially invested in it, or an amount that is as near to the original amount as feasible.

It's possible to make a livelihood off of selling butterflies; at least, that's what one gentleman discovered after someone wagered against him that he couldn't sell them. Not only did he come out on top in that wager, but he also built a successful enterprise on the strength of that one simple concept.

Check your recollection to see if you can unearth a concept that is buried deep within you that no one else would ever think could be successful in the context of an online business. There are a lot of other concepts that people have developedand made work successfully in that context. It is possible that this will demonstrate to them that they are incorrect...

Marketing Your Online Business Strategies for Success

After learning about a variety of online businesses from which you can choose, the next step is to educate yourself on the best practices for marketing your company so that it can achieve the same level of success as the businesses owned by many other internet marketers who have already traveled the path that you intend to follow.

Let's take a look at some of the most common approaches to marketing your web business.

Website

Your company's website, which is accessible over the internet, is an excellent starting point. The website itself is the single most important factor that will determine the success or failure of your company. The following is a list of information pertaining to your website that is essential to be aware of for the purposes of marketing:

Name of the Website's Domain A website's domain name is its address on the World Wide Web. It is important that the domain name you choose correspond closely to the name of your website or company. When looking for information on a specific subject, users of the internet will have an easier time locating your company thanks to this. If you are unable to locate a solution that is an exact match, you should look for an alternative that is as similar as feasible.

Keywords: Ensure that you make use of the most effective keywords when writing the content for your website. Internet users who are looking for information on a specific subject will type particular words into the search engines known as keywords. The search engine would then index the keywords and place them into the results page for a user to see. When a user sees your website higher up on the list of results, there is a greater likelihood that they will select it as the one they want to visit.

Market with a Specialty Focus Your company can target a more specific demographic of customers by developing a market niche for its products or services. concentrating your marketing efforts on a more select group in order to better meet the needs of your customers by doing so. Larger organizations have a greater number of members, each of whom has their own unique requirements. Because of this, it is challenging to pique the attention of your audience in what you have to offer. Marketing to the smaller groups will be lot simpler as they will consist of individuals who are more inclined to want what you have to offer.

Whatever target market you decide to focus on for your company, the website you build will need to reflect that. Your website should convey that message if you're going after mothers who already have young children. You would have images that would connect to women who have small children, and the material on the site should be written to something that they could relate to. In addition, the search engines will benefit from this change.

Blog - Include a blog as an additional feature on your website. It should be connected to the overall theme that your company's website has. Personal weblogs are not appropriate for this setting. If you use a blogging platform that isn't integrated with your website, you should make an effort to create the template of your blog to be as similar to your company website as is humanly possible. This will give the impression that the blog is an extension of the website.

Blogs are yet another method for utilizing search engines to bring in site visitors. When a visitor comes across your blog, they are able to see that you have more information to offer them on that subject elsewhere on your website; hence, they are able to simply click through on the link that is provided to continue reading.

E-Mail Marketing

E-mails are an important component of any marketing effort. This way, your company and its wares will remain in the minds of your prospective clients for as long as possible. It's one thing to attract a visitor to your website; it's quite another to make them remember you above the millions of other websites out there, particularly when they're in the market to make a purchase.

E-mails are sent out at predetermined intervals to deliver information to website visitors. This not only helps to develop credibility, but it also brings the name of your company to the forefront of their minds. There are a few distinct approaches one can take to accomplish this goal. People will be able to sign up for updates on what you are offering or for additional information using an opt-in email function that will be available on your website. This will enable you to collect e-mail addresses to whom you may send your communications.

Providing brief articles on a variety of subjects that are pertinent to your company is the purpose of newsletters. If you sell vitamins and minerals, for instance, you may demonstrate the significance of your product to potential customers by including articles in your newsletter that discuss various alternative health practices and the like.

It is possible to deliver to their inboxes newsletters that contain the beginning of an article together with a link that directs readers to your website, where they may finish reading the piece. This allows consumers to grow familiar with your site and makes it easier for them to remember you should they decide in the future that they want to purchase something that you are offering.

E-Courses enable site users to acquire foundational knowledge on a variety of subjects through the use of a sign-up function that may be placed on the website. If you offer vitamin goods, you may utilize an online course to help educate your customers about how to choose the most effective supplements to address a variety of health concerns.

E-courses are often delivered over the course of a week to seven days and are frequently made available at no cost. This helps to maintain your company's name in their heads by bringing it to their attention on a daily basis when the e-course is delivered to their inboxes.

Updates: You have the ability to send consumers who have purchased something from you or who have signed up for this feature updates on your products as well as discounts, freebies, and other promotional offers. If you do not succeed in persuading a customer to make a purchase on their initial visit, there is still a chance that they will do so during a subsequent visit if they come across anything that piques their interest and convinces them to make a purchase.

Your website may potentially see an increase in traffic as a result of the updates. Those individuals who have previously subscribed to your lists will have friends, family members, neighbors, and coworkers who they may refer to your company by simply forwarding the messages on to them.

Articles and Other Written Content

Besides providing good website content, articles and other written content can be used in several ways to market your business. Here are some of those ways:
Articles directories- Article directories provide great marketing tactics to use for your business. By writing and submitting an article related to your business site, you can achieve two things…

1. Credibility in the topic you have written about

2. Drive more traffic to your site by providing a link to your business website in the author's bio section provided on the article directory sites.

These directory sites usually rank well with the search engine results page, so someone stumbling upon one of your articles submitted within a directory can find their way over to your website for more information on that topic.

Articles placed within other site's newsletters or blogs- By being a guest writer on someone else's blog or newsletter, you can reach a whole other group of people looking for information on one topic.

You would provide a link to your site within these articles and then reciprocate the favor for the other website owner to provide the same kind of articles on your newsletters or blogs.

Articles on Digg or similar sites- Having one of your articles submitted on Digg or a similar type site will gain you more access to your site. Digg is a site that provides articles other internet users have deemed as good informative articles. Those articles that receive a large number of "Diggs" will be pushed to the home page where a lot of users will see and review them. Your site link could be included for those people who want more information on the topic.

Offer E-books or Guides- These can provide your consumers with information on a topic while including a link back to your site to keep them familiar with your business. These can be offered for free or for a small fee.
The word Free can be a powerful word to any user and catch their attention quite easily. You would provide some basic information on a topic and could get them interested in buying an e-Book that has more in-depth information about the same topic.

Socializing for Marketing

Spending time in the company of people who share your values and perspectives is one of the most effective strategies for increasing the number of people who visit your website because they are interested in the products or services you provide. The following is a list of the most common ways to interact with people in order to fulfill your requirements for marketing:

Commenting on blogs: Look for other blogs that cover a subject that is comparable to the one on your website. Make a comment in response to some of the postings that they've made. Because the link to your website will be connected to your name, people who are interested in learning more about the subject in question will look at your website or blog to see what you can provide for them.

Participate in online community discussion forums. Discover communities on message boards that discuss issues pertinent to your website and join them. Your website link could be included in the signature line, making it easier for other people to locate your site and check out what you have to offer there. First, you should look into the policies of the board to see if something like this is permitted.

You may establish your authority as an expert on the subject matter by participating in these forums on a consistent basis and gaining the trust of potential customers who are considering making a purchase from you. This will help you build credibility. In addition, the other board members may direct people they know to your website; hence, you should ensure that you give back as least as much as you receive inside these communities.

Websites That Are Used For Social Networking The term "social networking sites" refers to a wide variety of websites, including the immensely popular MySpace and Facebook. People who are interested in finding individuals who share their passions and interests are likely to frequent these websites. Internet marketers make frequent use of them in order to establish connections with members of the audience they are attempting to reach. People that share the same interests as you are able to communicate with you and begin to develop a sense of trust in you. They are more likely to do business with someone who is part of their "group," and they are also more likely to share information about your company with other people they know who might be interested.

Miscellaneous Marketing Techniques

The following are some other strategies that you might implement in your various marketing campaigns:

Affiliate Programs - Get the ball rolling on your product-related affiliate programs. Give other individuals the opportunity to profit from the sale of your products by doing it on their behalf. The efforts of another party will result in an increase in the amount of traffic that visits your website.

Find out how to develop your own successful affiliate program, and then create a web page on your website where other people may sign up to become your affiliates. You may choose to make an announcement regarding this matter in either your newsletters or your update messages.

Adwords is a service that search engines provide to business owners so that they can purchase advertising space on the sites that display the search results. You will be required to pay the search engine a particular sum of money each time one of your ads is selected by a user to be displayed.

Because you are paying for the clicks, you will want to create the most appealing advertisement that you can in order to maximize the return on investment that you receive. When you have poor advertisements, you run the risk of losing money because not all of the people who click on those advertisements will actually end up making a purchase. Maintain a record of these advertisements, and if necessary, remove them from circulation or rework them in order to prevent your company from suffering an excessive amount of financial loss. Campaigns based on word-of-mouth interaction are among the most

straightforward forms of marketing there are. People will talk about your company if you run a straightforward campaign to get the word out about it. This will lead to more people hearing about it, which will lead to more people hearing about it, and so on.

This is a terrific way for local consumers and clients to learn about your company and recommend it to others who might be looking for the same products or information. The marketing of your company can be accomplished in a cost-effective manner using this method as well.

Utilize Press Releases: You can utilize this strategy if you are simply opening your doors, if you are providing a discount or special sale, or if you are giving something else entirely. Users of the internet who are looking for particular information will find Press Releases published on websites after they have been submitted to those websites.

They are written in the style of a news article, and they feature your "news" by highlighting information and eye-catching headlines that grab people's attention and make them want to read more. Your new company venture, sale, or discount would receive a significant amount of exposure to those who have the potential to become customers.

It's possible that all you need is a well-written press release to advertise what it is that you are selling in order to attract a significant volume of people to the website of your company. Think about doing this on a regular basis so that people will continue to remember your company's name even after they've forgotten about it.

Put an ad in the newspaper that's circulated in your area. There's no rule that says you can't market your business in other ways besides the internet. Why not give local marketing a shot by advertising in the periodicals that are circulated in your community? The vast majority of people who live in that area and buy a copy of that publication are exposed to such adverts.

It's not uncommon for local clients to provide a company with their first taste of financial success, so when you're designing your marketing strategy, don't forget about the areas in your immediate vicinity.

Podcasting- Podcasting is a sort of audio material that people use to deliver information to other people in the form of an audio file that they listen to instead of reading. It presents them with an opportunity to learn about a subject that they are interested in through a different media. People really like the fact that they can download a podcast to their computer and listen to it while they are working on other things, so they don't have to stare at the screen all the time.

When people hear positive things about your company, they are more likely to trust it and regard it as credible. These listeners have the potential to become consumers for your business, and thus, your website will be linked to the radio program.

Marketing On The Fun Side

People are always looking for ways to lighten up and have a good time, so why not cater to that need with your marketing strategies? You can present it to them in a number of different ways, including the following:

Conduct a competition: When it is announced that there will be a competition, people will go from far and wide to participate. In order to increase the number of visitors to your blog or website, you should run one. In order for people to become aware of the competition, you will need to engage in a significant amount of marketing efforts; nevertheless, once they are aware, they will rush to participate.

Your competition should be one that is entertaining and open to the participation of virtually anybody. Provide a prize that is of significant value to the individual who wins the competition. If you don't do this, people won't rush to participate the next time you hold a contest or do anything else for your company.
A contest could consist of multiple-choice questions to be answered, an online scavenger hunt to explore different websites, or even just a simple lottery to select winners.

Have Products for promotional use that feature your company's brand can be fabricated by websites such as Cafe Press. These websites can create items such as T-shirts, pens, mugs, and even hats with your company's logo printed on them. Some of them could be presented to customers as presents, while others could be offered for sale on the website, where customers could make their purchases through a link that you provided.

These promotional goods could be placed in such a way that everybody who comes into contact with them will see your logo and be inquisitive about the company whose logo is on them. After that, they can conduct a search on your website to learn more about the products and services that you provide.

Ending Thoughts

A successful online business may be run by virtually anyone, regardless of how much prior experience that person may or may not have had in the commercial world. You don't really need much more than the desire to be successful, the ability to put in a lot of effort, and the willingness to learn as much as you can about the field of business that you decide to go into.

Because there is such a wide variety of possibilities available for online businesses, you should be able to choose one that is suitable for your requirements and the expertise that you can contribute to the venture. Employ any and all marketing strategies at your disposal to expand the reach of your company's online presence to every nook and cranny of the internet and to increase the amount of visitors who come to your website.

The effort and sweat that you put into it in the beginning will be worth it in the end because you will be able to start to relax a little and maybe employ someone else to do some of the everyday activities that you have been doing for yourself. What could possibly be a more efficient way to make a living than to pay someone else to perform the menial tasks that you despise doing yourself?

Why wait to jump on the bandwagon and start reaping some of the advantages that other online marketers are achieving when the internet continues to present business owners with more and more options to make money every single day? If they were able to achieve their goals despite having limited expertise in the business world, then you should have the same level of success.